SEA EMPRESS DISASTER

Chris Ogden

Illustrated by Karen Edward

OXFORD
UNIVERSITY PRESS

OXFORD
UNIVERSITY PRESS

Great Clarendon Street, Oxford OX2 6DP

Oxford University Press is a department of the University of Oxford.
It furthers the University's objective of excellence in research, scholarship,
and education by publishing worldwide in

Oxford   New York

Auckland   Cape Town   Dar es Salaam   Hong Kong   Karachi
Kuala Lumpur   Madrid   Melbourne   Mexico City   Nairobi
New Delhi   Shanghai   Taipei   Toronto

With offices in

Argentina   Austria   Brazil   Chile   Czech Republic   France   Greece
Guatemala   Hungary   Italy   Japan   Poland   Portugal   Singapore
South Korea   Switzerland   Thailand   Turkey   Ukraine   Vietnam

Oxford is a registered trade mark of Oxford University Press
in the UK and in certain other countries

British Library Cataloguing in Publication Data

Data available

ISBN-13:   978 0 19 919626 5
ISBN-10:   0 19 919626 5

7 9 10 8 6

Mixed Pack (1 of 6 different titles): ISBN-13: 978 0 19 919632 6; ISBN-10: 0 19 919632 X
Class Pack (6 copies of 6 titles): ISBN-13: 978 0 19 919631 9; ISBN-10: 0 19 919631 1

Illustrated by Karen Edward and David Russell
Cover photo by Marcel Mochet/Agence France Presse

Acknowledgements
pp 4/5 Photolibrary Wales; pp 6/7 Times Newspapers Ltd (TIM)/Rex Features;
p 12 Jones David Jones/Press Association; p 13 Dylan Garcia/Still Pictures;
p 18 Chinch Gryniewicz; Ecoscene/CO/Corbis UK Ltd.; p 19 Robin
Chittenden/Corbis UK Ltd.; pp 22/23 Phil Rees/Swansea – Dragon News;
p 24 Robert Eames/Impact Photos; p 25 RogerTidman/Corbis UK Ltd.;
p 27 Edward Parker/Still Pictures; p 30 Michael Busselle/Corbis UK Ltd.;
p 33 Hellier Mason/Still Pictures; p 34 Chinch Gryniewicz/Corbis UK Ltd.;
p 42 Tony Wharton/Fran/Corbis UK Ltd.; pp 42/43 Corel; p 43 Paul Kay/Oxford
Scientific Films; pp 44/45 Corel; pp 46/47 Corel

Printed in China by Imago

Contents

The characters in this story are fictional but the actual events of the *Sea Empress* disaster in 1996 are true and affected the lives of many people living or working in South Wales.

Introduction

My name is Ceri Thomas. I'm ten years old and I live near Milford Haven in South Wales. My dad's a fisherman. He catches sea bass and lobsters and sells them locally.

Mum works on the checkouts at our local supermarket, but I'd rather carry on the family tradition of fishing for a living and maybe even own my own boat one day!

The area we live in is very beautiful. The coastline has several **sites of special scientific interest**. We've got sandy and shingle beaches, rocky outcrops and tall towering cliffs and loads of birds come to breed on the islands in the coastal waters.

One of the worst things about living here is the oil tankers. They bring crude oil to the **refineries** in Milford Haven where it's turned into petrol. We all live in fear of an oil spill like the *Braer* in Scotland or the *Torrey Canyon*, which sank off the Cornish coast. The effects on the wildlife were terrible.

This is my diary of the events that followed a disaster with a tanker called the *Sea Empress* and how my family was affected.

The photograph in the background shows the typical scenery around the Carmarthen Bay area, where Ceri comes from.

CHAPTER

Friday
16th February

Onlookers watching the rescue operation

FRIDAY 16 FEBRUARY 1996

Western Mail

SUPERSHIP RUNS AGROUND

AN ENVIRONMENTAL DISASTER LOOKS INEVITABLE after the single-hulled *Sea Empress* with 131,000 tonnes of crude oil aboard, ran aground outside Milford Haven at 8.07pm last night.

The weather was calm and visibility was good as the supertanker made its way towards Milford Haven.

Early reports indicate that around 2,500 tonnes of crude oil have leaked into the sea as the vessel remains stuck on a sandbank.

Mum and I met Dad early this morning at the harbour and helped him take his catch to the fish market. It was all shut up. Typical!

We took the fish round to some of the local shops where he sells his lobsters. None of the owners would buy his fish. I didn't understand until Dad told me the terrible news about a tanker that's run aground. The *Sea Empress* is leaking **crude oil** into the waters of Carmarthen Bay where Dad and his mates go fishing.

Dad says a salvage team is planning to pump the remaining oil into another ship and tow the *Sea Empress* into Milford Haven. Mum didn't say a word as we travelled back.

Mum cooked some of the fish for our breakfast but none of us felt like eating! Dad got cross and said that the fish was perfectly safe to eat. So why didn't anyone want to buy it?

Went to school hungry with no tuck money! Unfair!

The weather became worse this morning. Mrs Howells, our headteacher, took us out in the wind and rain. We all stood in the playground as she pointed at the sea.

A Dakota aircraft sprays the growing oil slick with special chemicals to help break it up

Our school's on a hill so we can look down at the ships as they travel to and from Milford Haven. I thought Mrs Howells had gone mad 'til I saw what everyone else was staring at. There was a large, dark, black patch on the water, which stretched as far as we could see. Mrs Howells said it was the beginning of an oil slick from the tanker.

The sign says it all...

Arrived home just as it began to rain harder. I heard Mum and Dad in the living room arguing. Mum said she hadn't got enough money to pay the rent. Dad said it wasn't his fault and switched on the television. Mum switched it off.

I took a packet of crisps from the kitchen and went up to my bedroom out of their way. I hate it when they argue!

CHAPTER

2

**Saturday
17th February**

Watched the news on the TV this morning. The newsreader said the government has put a 'Closure Order' along our coastline. It means that none of the fishermen are allowed to catch any fish or crabs or lobsters. That includes Dad! He seemed really cross about it. I'd have thought he'd be glad of the rest.

Normally he moans when he has to go fishing in bad weather.

Mum explained to me that Dad might be fined if he catches any fish. And even if he caught lobsters or crabs, no one would buy them because the oil pollution makes them poisonous. I was glad we didn't eat the fish yesterday!

Put my waders on and went with Dad down to the beach. It was horrible! All the golden sand has been covered with a thick blanket of sticky, black oil. The smell was awful. Lots of people were trying to clean up the mess.

Volunteers help members of the Marine Pollution Control Unit to clean up the beach

Dad and I walked along the **strandline** looking for creatures that might have been washed up. We found one or two dead birds that were coated in oil. Dad said we should help scrape the oil off the rocks but then I saw a blackened wing flapping from amongst the seaweed. It was a guillemot and it was still alive – just!

An oil covered guillemot

Dad and I carried it to a cleaning station that had been set up nearby. I asked if I could help. A lady called Helen gave me some charcoal and fish, which I fed to my bird. One of the

volunteers washing the birds with soapy water said that charcoal helps get rid of any oil in the bird's stomach. The guillemot tried to eat a couple of pieces but he was very weak. I decided to call him Gazza.

Dad went back to help clean the oil off the sand. I wondered what Mum would say when she found out he'd been helping the clean-up operation instead of earning money.

CHAPTER

Sunday 18th February

The ship struggles in high seas

SUNDAY 18 FEBRUARY 1996

Western Mail

SECOND SLIP FOR SUPER-SHIP

In a Force 9 gale and with high, strong-running tides, the crew of the doomed ship, the *Sea Empress*, were winched to safety by helicopter. Earlier, tugs had managed to get a line to the stricken ship but the *Sea Empress* broke free and became stuck on rocks near St Anne's Head.

It is thought that 20,000 tonnes of crude oil have already leaked into Carmarthen Bay.

Many of the beautiful beaches along this part of South Wales are already covered in oil and thousands of seabirds and creatures are believed to be in danger.

Watched the news again this morning. There were more pictures of the *Sea Empress* as it was battered by the wind and waves. Important-looking people discussed what the disaster would mean to the area.

Dad went to see his mate, Gareth, to see what he was going to do for work.

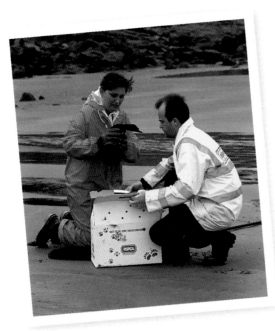

Continuing to rescue helpless birds

Went down to the beach rescue centre, in the rain, to see Gazza. There were lots of other birds there but Gazza has been transferred to a centre in Milford Haven. I was really disappointed. Helen said that they were hoping to release him when he's stronger.

RSPCA members removing oil from a Black Scoter

When Dad came back tonight, he said he and Gareth had taken their boats out and towed long booms across several of the local beaches and harbours to try and stop the oil slick washing inland. Mum didn't say anything!

A boom protects the beach from the oil

CHAPTER

4

Monday 19th February

Watched the pictures on breakfast TV of yesterday's attempt by the tugs to keep the *Sea Empress* in one place as they battled against a Force 9 gale. The ship became stuck on other rocks and the engine room flooded.

Mrs Howells asked us to collect old sheets and washing-up liquid to give to the bird cleaners. School finished at lunchtime today because everyone was helping with the clean-up operation. Great!

Aunt Lorna, Mum's sister, rang tonight. She runs a hotel in Tenby. She told Mum

Tenby

that oil has been washed up on the sandy beaches and stuck all over the rocks. People have been ringing all day to cancel their holidays because of the pollution and she's even had to send some of her staff home.

Mum tried to sound sympathetic but I could see she was becoming crosser with Aunt Lorna. Mum told her that Dad isn't able to earn any money. It sounds like Mum's been trying to get some extra hours at the

shop but the manager's told her that
he can't afford to pay her. Mum's voice
went really quiet but I still heard what
she said. A tear rolled down her cheek
and fell onto an open, brown envelope
on the table. It looked like another
bill. Now I know we're in trouble.
Mum never cries!

Tuesday 20th February

Dad found some work helping with the clean-up operation. He sprayed chemicals over the rocks to break up the oil.

Continuing the
clean-up operation

On tonight's news they said that 50,000 tonnes of oil have escaped today. I thought of all those poor helpless fish and stranded birds struggling to stay alive. It made me think of Gazza. I wondered how he was recovering at the centre in Milford Haven.

CHAPTER

Wednesday 21st February

Success! The ship has been refloated. Gareth rang Dad to tell him the news. Twelve tugs towed it into Milford Haven. At last it looks like the disaster is finally over. Perhaps now things will get back to normal.

Two of the tugs help to secure the oil tanker

Mum's been looking for more work but no one can afford to pay her. Dad spent the day hosing oil off the rocks with a jet spray. He wasn't paid for doing it and Mum said he was stupid! Dad threw his oily boots on the floor and said he was sick and tired of her moaning. He went to bed. I didn't know what to say to either of them.

Thursday 22nd February

Woke up. Mum had some bad news
for me! Dad is leaving home for a few
weeks.

I hope it's got nothing to do with all the arguments. He says he's going to try and find work in the dockyards at Bristol. Mum says they need some money quickly. Dad leaves tomorrow morning on the high tide.

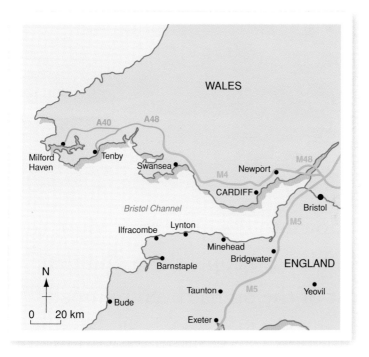

A map showing the location of Milford Haven in relation to Bristol

Friday 23rd February

Went down to the quay with Mum to
see Dad leave. People there said that
the last of the oil has been pumped
out of the *Sea Empress* but the clean-up
operation is still continuing and could
last for months.

I felt really sad as Dad's little fishing boat left the harbour and headed out to sea. Behind it towered the giant shape of the moored *Sea Empress*, the cause of all our troubles. Mum had a tear in her eye.

Suddenly a guillemot swooped low over Dad's head and circled for a moment. I realised that it wasn't Gazza but I felt sure it was a sign that things were going to get better. As Dad's boat became a tiny dot on the waters of the bay, I knew in my heart he'd return soon.

Creatures affected by the oil spill

common scoter

Spends the winter months 1–3km off the shore.

Food: shellfish and **crustaceans**

cormorant

Black and very dark green plumage, white chin.

Food: fish and eels

razorbill

Black plumage, white underparts, white grooved lines under the bill.

Food: fish

Razorbill

guillemot

Very dark plumage, white underparts.
Food: fish for which it dives and swims
with its wings underwater

lobster

Caught in pots sunk on the surface of
the sea

edible crab

Caught on a
line or in traps
similar to
lobster pots

Edible crab

sea bass

Found in the coastal
waters off South Wales

limpets

Molluscs that cling tightly to rocks

Disaster Factfile

 The *Sea Empress* disaster was the third worst in British maritime history.

 It took 12 tugs and six days before the tanker was finally recovered and towed into Milford Haven.

 A total of 73,450 tonnes of oil were lost in the disaster.

 More than 280km of coastline were affected by the oil, including 35 Sites of Special Scientific Interest.

 Large quantities of contaminated sand were removed – up to 1,000 tonnes from Pendine Sands.

⚠ Oil was still being washed ashore 4 months later.

⚠ The chemical **dispersants** used to break up the oil slick actually increased the ecological damage.

⚠ Farmers reported seeing an oily film on their animals drinking water. This had been blown inland by the winds.

⚠ It took five years for the shellfish and crustaceans to recover.

⚠ 16–20,000 seabirds were killed including guillemots and razorbills.

⚠ 35 seals were seen covered in oil.

⚠ Large numbers of limpets and starfish died.

⚠ 90% of the Common Scoter duck population were affected. 53% died.

⚠ Poisonous **hydrocarbons** are still present in the oil that was lost. These can cause cancer and other diseases in fish and shellfish as well as sea mammals like seals, whales, dolphins, and porpoises.

⚠ Commercial fisheries worth 3 million pounds were affected over five years.

⚠ Between 34 and 48 million pounds in compensation was supposed to have been paid to the fishing and tourist industries.

⚠ Many people were ill after contact with the oil, but no-one ate any poisoned fish.

⚠ The accident was caused by an inexperienced **pilot** bringing the **supertanker** into Milford Haven. It was therefore the Port Authority who were found to be responsible They were fined 4 million pounds.

⚠ The total cost of the disaster is estimated to have been 64 million pounds.

⚠ There is always the risk that another disaster may happen.

Index

Glossary

crude oil untreated, thick, black oil

crustaceans creatures with hard shells, e.g. crabs

dispersants chemicals used to break up thick oil

hydrocarbon a poisonous, chemical compound

pilot a person who navigates ships in and out of port

pollution anything that makes an environment harmful

refinery a place where crude oil is turned into other products like petrol

site of special scientific interest (SSSI) a place that has rare flowers, rocks or creatures and needs to be protected

strandline the line of seaweed and debris left behind by the tide

supertanker a large ship carrying oil or other liquids